Little Knitted Sister

THE RAGGED SKY POETRY SERIES

The Luxury of Obstacles
by Elizabeth Danson

Little Knitted Sister
by Ellen Foos

Moonmilk and Other Poems
by Carlos Hernández Peña

Between Silence and Praise
by Elizabeth Anne Socolow

Escape Velocity
by Arlene Weiner

ELLEN FOOS

Little Knitted Sister

RAGGED SKY PRESS

PRINCETON • NEW JERSEY

Published by Ragged Sky Press
270 Griggs Drive
Princeton, NJ 08540

Library of Congress Cataloging-in-Publication Data

Foos, Ellen, 1955-
Little knitted sister / Ellen Foos. — 1st ed.
p. cm. — (The Ragged Sky poetry series)
ISBN-13: 978-0-9633092-5-9 (pbk.)
ISBN-10: 0-9633092-5-0 (pbk.)
I. Title. II. Series.

PS3606.O66L58 2006
811'.6—dc22 2005030242

Some of the poems in this book originally appeared in the following publications: *Edison Literary Review, U.S. 1 Worksheets, Kelsey Review,* and *Sensations Magazine.*

This book is composed in Gotham and Minion

Text and cover design by Foos Rowntree
Cover art: detail of *L#5,* 2004, oil on canvas, 24"x18" by Jean Foos

Manufactured in the United States of America

First Edition

ELLEN FOOS grew up in Rochester, New York and then embarked on a career in publishing. She is currently a production editor at Princeton University Press. A member of U.S. 1 Poets' Cooperative, she leads a monthly reading series for the group and also organizes poetry slams with the local arts council.

Contents

❁ Farmer Green's Fresh Brown Eggs 1
The Porridge Is Cold 2
Church Music 3
Drowned Virgins 4
The Wedding Feast at Fairport 5
Holy Week in Nicaragua 6
Beehive 7
Hospital Birthday 8
Wayne & Elaine 9
Instant Message 10
Chronic Calls 11
Staging Area 12
Man with a Broken Nose 13

❁❁ Little Knitted Sister 17
In the Sand Pile 18
Car Repair 19
Blessings 20
Maternal Instinct 21
Beatitude 22
Whistling Girls 23
Painter in the Family 24
The Poet Who Wanted to Be a Zookeeper 25
Where to Find Her 26
Daughter to Mother 27
Go Tell Aunt Rhody 28
The Madwoman 29
Madness or Chocolate 30

Pained Awareness 31
Carrot 32
Dream 33
Cats at the Ballgame 34
If I Had a Penis 35
Fear of Sunsets 36
Turning the Bed Down 37
At Home in Boots 38
Mountaintop 39
At Ease 40

❀❀❀ Dark Weather 43
Moths in the Crackers 44
Where the Ferry Took You 45
The Transmigration of Souls through Waxed Paper 46
Red Bird, Green Willow 47
Great Blue over Griggs Farm 48
Sycamore in the Rain 49
Ed's Day at the Beach 50
Flash 51
Glass Arbor 52
Watering 53
Snowbound 54
Deer Leg 55

Farmer Green's Fresh Brown Eggs

A slippery jelly clings to the cracked shell
as an egg is turned inside out.

The morning has found its mooring
settling into an iron frying pan.

Dazed, we all chose olive oil
when butter lost its glow,

but chickens can't be jollied
into heart-safe yolk.

Give us this day our daily bread
in the form of toast

that laps up the last smear
of eggs-over-easy.

I found love in a roadside diner
where it was breakfast served all day.

The Porridge Is Cold

For somebody who was out dancing all night,
what did you expect?

No princes turned up while you were gone;
the bears are in their usual bad mood.

Your hair could use a color rinse
and that robe's a bit frumpy.

Nobody waltzes away from disaster like you
but this once I think you should take inventory.

A bed and a few chairs aren't enough to make a life.

Church Music

What wafts outside is coated in butter,
a Sunday taste of consolation
as we walk to the holy-water font,
shoes laced with sharp precision.

A row of backs in the last pew
shades the doorway where
fluffs of high notes leak
into the uncrowded street.

Groaning sounds from
Miss Pickney's indulgent
organ carry
a mile to the drugstore.

Hands lift at the swell
of rhythm and blues
anchored in release,
bread on the table.

Drowned Virgins

They lie at the bottom of the sea,
water lilies that sank
before they flowered,
anxious to please but unable
to deliver—

too proud, too afraid,
too quintessentially pure.
We're dredging them up now because
they are back in demand—
boys who never got started,
girls who never went all the way.

If we give them another chance
they'll happily drop their conceit,
knowing how dim the light is,
how cold the sandy bed,
down in the lonely channels of the Atlantic.
How much better to tread the mucky earth.

The Wedding Feast at Fairport

A blush falls over the crowd,
the bouquet so rich, the rosé so pink.
Wine pours out like the Red Sea,
the waters part and join again
what no man shall put asunder.

Fearing a last minute judgment,
the groom wonders if he should have done more
to help with the plans.
The bride realizes it will always be like this.
And it's not the first time for either of them.

Maybe an attempt to keep the ex out of the obituary
or the kids from moving back in.
They'll all be there anyway,
sucking down mixed drinks
while the Lord is in the basement
doing His work.

A good guest stays to help clean up
but often you can't last that long.

Holy Week in Nicaragua

for Father Bill Daniel, 1926–2002

A year ago we were shoveling sand
from the riverbank
into your Kia pickup truck.
Dry-season flowers were in bloom.
Processions formed outside every church.
Our labor meant another block house
would appear in a landscape
of plastic-bag shacks.

Your trademark of simple stained glass
offered a window of hope.

Only twelve months later
a brick in a human hand
has been laid hard against your head.
Vengeance divided a minister with very little
from a neighbor with no reserves.

Rebirth is unlikely out of such dust
although you have surprised us before.

Beehive

The worst moment came
when the furious buzzing stopped,
a hive crumpled in on itself,
silence from the interior.

Such a fragile concentration of industry,
queen, honey, drones, all gone.
The crushed remains become
their own burial ground.

Battlefields are not this compact
and flower fields are not this gray.
In the predatory world it is safer
to spread out now—
to leave the dead behind.

Hospital Birthday

In a bed of electric signals
you lie where life is guarded.
Seventy years are counted

but candles aren't allowed.
So we burn them briefly
and sing like bandits.

Your close-cropped hair flashes youth.
Something spiritual surrounds your oddness
before you dash on new eyebrows.

An aging cat, a feckless son
vaguely call you home.
The food is better here,

the room so tidy.
Television is the same
no matter where you watch it.

Wayne & Elaine

They are willing to walk around the long way
together, rather than in separate anxious states.
Wayne moderates powerful cravings,
trusting Elaine will understand his limits.
She teaches difficult children; he's
a psychologist. Both have seen deep
into troubled pasts and recognize their own.

The un- couple, unassuming, unpretentious,
with a calm assurance, tempered by life's unbalances,
ready to meet each other on neutral ground,
contained by each other's sturdy affection.
They live a small town life, moving on a surface
that's been cleared, like snow off a frozen pond.
The whole world merges to keep them steady.

Instant Message

Light a candle, quench a fire.
Burn your draft card.
Wave the flag.

Visit the wall of noise.
Recognize some glyph
that is scribbled there.

Sign up for extra minutes.
Decode the hidden meaning.
Connect with alien beings.

March on Washington.
Protest anonymity.
Sing for New York.

Be a child no longer.
Operate on your last dime.
Spare the oratory.

This is the last message
before the rates go up.
Write back if you get a chance.

Chronic Calls

Daily I hear the phone
wailing for my hand on its backside.

Misplaced from the wall base,
it wanders into the kitchen from
the TV room. There are fundraisers
standing by to take my pledge.

Hello, I cry, why are you calling?
This is my lost world of voices
unyielding to the hunger for dinner.

But it's never allowed to leave the house,
take a ride to the grocery aisle where
it would offer remote shopping decisions.

No wonder it hates to be quiet just when I'm leaving
and stands blinking in one-eyed confusion
when I return.

Staging Area

Are they putting on a play?
In a way.

Will there be lights?
Sure, infra-red.

Sound effects?
Your eardrums will shatter.

Costumes?
Camouflage.

Special effects?
Bullets and blood.

Box-office stars?
Nobody you've heard of.

Man with a Broken Nose

—Rodin Museum, Philadelphia

Brotherly love was not this man's fate,
whose visage is modeled beside Balzac's,
here in this stately museum.

Rodin saw something new,
the beauty of a fracture,
a face with a story.

Philadelphia dresses itself
in the grand old style,
though its bumps are evident.

Granite walls and a reflecting pool
give shade to
a homeless encampment.

An unlucky starling
does a frantic breaststroke
then climbs aboard an extended branch.

The rescuer observes
a purple radiance,
broken-winged but saved.

Little Knitted Sister

The Knit-Wits were a family.
Green father, blue mother,
pink and yellow children.
Yarn-topped heads.

The youngest child was good.
She did what she was told.
Got thrown across the playroom
and bounced right back.

The stuffed parents were
nonchalant. They'd go to the
seashore with Little Sister
locked in the toy cupboard.

Once the dog got her and left her
very worn down.
She spent the rest of the week
lying in the yard.

The yellow brother was okay.
He squashed her almost
inside out but then let her
wear his cowboy vest.

Nowadays plastic fashion
models don't have families.
The knitted sister was lucky
to grow up back then.

In the Sand Pile

Small armies went underground,
water flowed into trench strongholds,
our day stalled while a bare rock
made a big job for a Tonka truck.

Pant cuffs were sandbags until
emptied by a handstand.

The hill became a stage
for astonishing deformity,
groans of speechlessness,
dragging limbs and crossed eyes.

A bright anthem broke out:
Tah-rah-rah-boom-de-ay
we have no school today.

The littlest kid went in
for string to stake out quarters
where captive bugs mixed
with miniature farm animals

and war settled into peace.

Car Repair

There we were on our gravel driveway,
two mechanics listening for a strange noise.
It was more of a puzzle to me than to my dad.
If I stood aside when he opened the hood
and didn't expect answers to my chatter,
we got along fine.

A trip to the shop was rare—
his worker's hands could fix anything.
I picked at rust and dug for change in the seats,
played with the monkey wrench.
It was too dull for anyone else in the family,
or they wouldn't risk a lecture.

My father took out the army blanket
to lie down for a closer look.
I hung around while half of him disappeared,
watched black ants crawl on his legs.
We were a team that could easily break up
by the end of the day or the end of the summer.

Blessings

One has to live a long time to reach eighty.
Enough days to go around the world.
You could have kept us kids
down on the farm
but you wanted a lot more.

The gray skies of Rochester
cover the brightest blooms.
Out beyond the yard there are
buildings going up.
With so many of us
there was no room to complain.

Now we've rounded up our riches
and found our way home,
hoping to satisfy a severe god.

None are dead, none are missing.
We're holding on for dear life
and looking back to see what fell out
because we used to ride
with the windows rolled down.

I'm here to feel the strength of the tribe.
We went to all this trouble after years
of taking orders, only to realize
we had the best father we could manage.

Maternal Instinct

Not a mother who drove us to things,
didn't like driving—or other Moms—
but in the backyard she neglected
her clothesline to play with us.
Joe was steady when she married him,
seven kids later he is still solid.
Her dreams were artistic,
not caught up in soap operas.
She was creating a new breed
with crayons, storybooks and blind faith.
We tried hard to satisfy;
her rovers, fakers and whiners,
scholars and volunteers.
On Sundays we went to Mass
and then for candy.
She kept her eye on the kitchen clock,
telling us the time
or teaching us to tell it.
Smell the pines she'd insist
when we were bundled on a walk.
It pierces me now
like no other advice.

Beatitude

Motherhood took hold like a raspberry bush,
rooted in encouragement, caution, and expectation.

A boy is wired for games of domination
boasting his way through endless rounds of sport,

but my son has a rulebook for every injustice,
a winning smile when the arrogant are undressed.

I turn out praise the way other mothers bake cookies,
sample a bit for myself, substitute if there's a shortage.

It's nice to be a saint in such a small church.
Miracles never debated, and my child so easy to give all for.

Whistling Girls

Whistling girls and cackling hens
always meet with some bad end.

Between the veils, the vows, the virgins,
whispers carry special orders
not to venture past the border.

Snow White sent the seven dwarfs
singing to their forest work:
the witch was on the way.

Once, I stood onstage and bowed
in my meekest good-girl pose.
Now behind the furthest curtain
I pucker up my lips and blow.
Not to kiss, but whistle, whistle, whistle.

Painter in the Family

Her splattered clothes resemble
the canvases she paints.
She lives on streets that smell like coffee,
her studio a linseed oil emporium.

Shy but determined, she stood out
in a crowd of eager children;
an art so real at first, then clearly abstract,
her Christmas paint set got bigger every year,

her colors bright as our RCA.
From amateur correspondence course to
nude models in high-ceilinged rooms,
then a leap into pure space,

our hope bigger than Dad's new car.
The city that lured her away, trapped her
into a scramble and a struggle of soul,
a style that registers as homesickness.

The Poet Who Wanted to Be a Zookeeper

It was a simple career-day choice
to find a handsomely uniformed outdoor job,
convince yourself that animals are fun and easy to care for,
know you don't ever want to sit behind a desk.
You already wear a school uniform—theirs at least has pants.

Out in the rain with a shovel
or strolling in the sun with a sack of feed,
speaking your mind without critical reply.
Not an unbearable vision, though
a bit fuzzy on home life—did one live at the zoo?

Where to Find Her

Singing her heart out,
she left work
to wander through meadows.

Where to find happiness
if not in the hills?
Birds flew over unnoticing,
her feet followed unmarked paths.
She couldn't be found.

Back home, a house
kept out earth and sky,
her voice seemed too loud.
In a flood of appreciation,
she decided to lie down outside the door.

Daughter to Mother

Well, Mom, I'll tell you,
what you never told me
I had to figure out for myself.

If you said it's too expensive,
I never bought one.
If you said don't try that,
I never did.

You never told me to speak
my mind,
you never told me some people
are mean,
you never told me to put on
a bit of a show, take a chance,
or let my hair grow. You never told me
being a girl was fun.

Go Tell Aunt Rhody

Just as my fertility was cycling out of existence
a plant in the corner of the bedroom
produced a shoot that flowered
into something toylike and overly fragrant.

Was this the death knell,
a corn plant's swan song?
But no, only a rare bloom of health.

Why sound the alarm over my budding predicament
when it's as familiar as a child's song?
Where only the goose ends up in the millpond.

The Madwoman

Doesn't want to live alone,
wishes children didn't grow up and leave.
She ambles through woods with open eyes
happy to face wild wind and rain,
but holds the brakes when biking downhill,
wonders if she's too lucky sometimes.

Friends once asked her why she was so quiet,
now she speaks too much, a weld unsealed;
and she'll tackle dirty windows just to lessen
the distance between inside and out.

Streaks of gray hair are a sure sign of lunacy,
if she keeps hers pulled back she can almost hide.
Discounts on bus fare mean a lot more trips,
there's no charge for changing direction now.
Her teeth still have some strength—
don't wait for her to bite into your skin.

Madness or Chocolate

Music plays in another room.
It snowed dispiritedly this morning,
the ground outside hard like stale bread.
I'm so sorry for wishing you somewhere else,
the furnace making my head heavy.

Chocolate is the only recourse.
Since the days of feeble Tootsie Rolls,
my enjoyment rides on sweetness.
To dig in a Christmas stocking
is not beyond reason.
I'll spit out a pink taffy center if I must.
It's a biological urge for survival—
one bag of M&Ms at a time.

Pained Awareness

A cranky nature and a sore knee
pull me down equally.
Both I have earned with intent,
striding to get somewhere.

Vowing to change my ways
helps, when I think of it.
I'll favor the other leg,
try being a little kinder.

But the suddenness of an open beach
stripped of all obstacles
undermines a sensible pace.
I charge along the sand.

Indoors, impatience prevails
against complacent coworkers
who barely pull themselves from their chairs.

The repair I seek is a form of reprieve.
Let me continue this way a little longer,
then I'll yield to the gnawing aches
that want me to be gentle.

Carrot

Crisper bin
though cold is deep
a carrot fades
in dreamy sleep.

Lettuce wilts
and onions rot,
a plastic net
contains their lot.

Rabbit hutch
or compost heap
are close at hand
when food won't keep.

Heads and hearts
and eyes and skin
turn to mold
in crisper bin.

Dream

A little hope, a little impossible casting
and a dance begins.

Happily, I know the steps.
Cruelly, the musicians disappear.

A long tunnel of travel and I find
the party has resumed outdoors.

I'll join in again if I can hide the blood-red
stains, the ancient underwear.

When I wake, relief and regret.

Nothing real destroyed,
nothing dreamlike attained.

Cats at the Ballgame

They purred for Mike Piazza,
hissed at the price of beer,
rubbed up against the ushers
for better seats.
Saw themselves on the big screen.

Fur flew when Mo Vaughn got out on a bad call;
the peanuts were too salty.
Naturally, these cats took
the seventh-inning stretch.
Guys in the row behind knew all the stats.

Fickle fans left at the end of the eighth,
but the cats held on,
hoping the southpaw would weaken
and the home team chase in some runs.
The three blind mice could call it a win.

If I Had a Penis

First I would see exactly how hard it would be
to pee straight into the bowl.

Then, will all my pants still fit
or will they bulge and bind?

That's assuming I got a big one, which
is another question to weigh.

I'm not inclined to take it on the town
but a self-induced foray

into sexual delight seems likely,
and I have some moves to try.

A few days are all I could take and then
it would have to come off,

and be hidden in a drawer until needed on hikes—
no squatting in the bushes again.

Fear of Sunsets

This could be the last time I sit at the keyboard
undoing the automatic cap at the beginning of each new line.
I might never again worry about the wrinkling wall over my dryer
that indicates moisture buildup from a faulty exhaust fan.

The sky is so beautiful right now, all color fading slowly
into a marsh of forgetfulness and abstraction.
There is no saving voice downstairs asking
if I want some tea or where did the *Weekend* section go.

If I die, no one will know my last thoughts.
How I noticed the veins in my hands disappeared
when I put them over my head. That I was aware
just how alive I was right before the end.

If I do see another sunset
I may not even notice
that I'm with you,
that it's night.

Turning the Bed Down

A daily chore presages the night.
Take a perfectly well-made bed,
fold back the top.

A courtesy and a welcome.
An old-fashioned busymaking
sign of passion.

How did I end up
with a grandma and a boyfriend
both so inclined?

At Home in Boots

Rugged suburbanite,
car-loving hiker, dog-loving cyclist,
on dreary days you go out,
sunny days you sleep in.

Music is your mother tongue
where the blues get their say.
You frequent doctors and mechanics
so what broke down will run again.

A classic cool-skinned reptile outside
but a case study in warmth
when your friends need a mammal.

I'll worry if you ever quit eating
or spruce up your wardrobe,
knowing you like things
filling and familiar.

Someday you'll have a long rest
up on Kimmel's hilltop
and everyone will stop wondering
when is he going to get here?

Meanwhile, I'm noticing
your one-hand, zigzag style
of tying up a new pair of boots.

Mountaintop

At night you wrap your bald head,
as if to contain the dome of cosmic confusion.

Gratitude sometimes scatters itself upon
the humble social worker.

Merlin removes his cap, uncertain at day's end
that his powers have done good.

You can be sure your magic
makes the world less raggedy.

At Ease

Round-bellied, calm-voiced—
a gourd left in the garden
long after the peas have been picked.

Today the wind is blowing
through the web of lawn chairs.
Come on, tell me a story
about when you made rockets.

Dark Weather

Under low clouds there's a sharp breeze,
the campus becomes quicker on its feet.

Shade trees standing for decades bend doubtfully.
Wondering, *When did the universe begin?*

Science labs glow more yellow,
reports advance after lingering all week.

Fossil finders sift through data,
calculating dinosaur advantages.

Ever so softly it begins to rain—
black umbrellas rise up, their ribs gone haywire.

Visitors are tagged and welcomed into stone passageways,
yesterday's coffee cups have been cleared.

Damp tones from keyboards and phones
distract the music theorists from their intervals.

Thunder or the rumbling of a superconductor
introduces a shifting performance.

A shuttle bus whiskers past on the roadway,
delivering reinforcements.

Moths in the Crackers

Persistent little insects,
opportunistic visitors,
in their larval or flying form—
cobwebs tell the tale:
something is in residence.

Even super vigilance
doesn't secure us from
these occasional invasions.

You can accidentally eat some,
or choose to eat around them,
or be so mortally bugged
that crackers and all dry goods
go right out the door.

There's always some suspicion—
so you're the first to see signs
in other people's cupboards.

It's not just the nightly news
or doctor's lab reports
that have us on edge—
we fear the microfauna in the kitchen.

Where the Ferry Took You

for Spalding Gray, 1941–2004

All this time you've been containing
the Monster in the Box
by talking about it.
Now it's out and you're gone with it.

You made everyone hear
about your mother's suicide,
so they'd respect the Monster.

Years ago I joined you onstage,
telling the audience about
my days as a lifeguard.

I'm bolder now, confessing publicly
to love and anger, but not to death.
I've drawn the line.
It's not in me to risk more than
minor embarrassment.

Your wry smile and lifted eyebrow—
so practiced and natural—
makes the truth easier to expose.
How can you show the center unless
you think it's beautiful too?

I want to learn to live with the Monster.
You followed your mother into the water.

The Transmigration of Souls through Waxed Paper

Light so dull, I can't see
beyond the first layer of the cookie tin.

Mercy on the lowest of the low,
dogs and squirrels closely aligned.
High hats for the obviously worthy.

What of my dying friend?
Soon to be on a waiting list
for Nepalese Sherpa, I am sure,
she hums in solitude against
a conviction that this is the last stop.

Time is a smooth shell,
a temporary lodging.
Not only bound to us but boundless,
a shallow grave for sudden revival.

Die in a fire and wake in a cradle.
Newborn eyes look inward,
wary of starting over.

Red Bird, Green Willow

In a drizzle of orderly lawns
without a surviving dandelion,
traffic hurling in the near distance,
sings the broadminded cardinal.

Hot diesel winds blow
through daggers of willow leaves.
Someone drags bottles to the curb
to wait for the pickup crew.

New asphalt forms a burnt crust.
Rocks bundled in wire
guard the slipping landscape.
A dog goes by in a backpack.

Great Blue over Griggs Farm

Looking for water, she finds none;
looking for a roost, only rooftops,
so she sails on—
long legs dangling like apron tails,
graceful matron on her way
to stalk a riverbed for food.
This heron shops for a quiet place
knowing my blue-gray satellite dish
collects no signals to help her find shoals to rest in.
Yet, no need to think she's lost—
crooked silhouette on a straight path;
she distantly grasps that this farm—
a crowded development, with sparrows
pecking out sustenance—offers
only grounds armored
against ponds and cornfields.
Under her passing shadow I long to follow.

Sycamore in the Rain

The hide brightens, yellow bark
has sheen, a value of gold
in the bare winter.

A glossy veneer
we wish for when it's dry
though we chafe when it's wet.

Give us our coins, exchange
this gloom for treasure,
a magic book brushed with water.

Ed's Day at the Beach

His first trek over the sand is cool.
Waves salt the air. A blanket
with a clear view is anchored
under shoes and bottled water.

The sun rises early and sets late.
Clouds must streak by quickly.
Fat women should hide under towels
and men keep their greasy snacks away.

When the chatter and heat build
a long swim makes it right again.
Now it's just a matter of lying
face down to invite the breeze.

Eventually he will get up
and walk down the shore,
past the flooded moats guarded
by plastic utensils.

Now children and dogs are packed
over the tar, into backseats
of departing cars. Suddenly the light
takes a new slant over the bowling ocean.

Flash

The roof leaks into pans,
the world is wet.
Gunnels ache
and slosh over.

Barn doors are broken,
going in or out.
Narrow escapes
are commonplace.

Summer is not safe
out on the golf greens.
The tax man, the lady chiropractor,
threaten at home.

Almighty wrath is
unleashed by childish acts.
You'll look older tomorrow
than magazines today predict.

Glass Arbor

I walk through sun-glazed topiary
where aloe quills and sugared lamb's ears
shelter a motionless luna moth.

A mourning dove worries along
the gravel path ahead of me.
I recognize a weathered bucket and imagine
mealy bugs moving underneath.

In this childhood garden, grown over
with years of inattention,
a blue hysteria conjures up
ancient burials, gleaming fountains.
Quietly, recollection rocks the archway.

Watering

Under the tap outside
a mossy bib covers the ground.
The seasonal drip not wasted,
a groan from the faucet handle
preserves this small oasis.

There hangs a changeable coil of hose,
sometimes twisted and stiff, today pliant
in the warm dusk, heavy even before it fills—
lifeline to the thirsty grass, the aging garden,
the dry dog bowl.

I grip the gunlike nozzle, recalling
high arcs with just my thumb, drenching
my sweaty playclothes when I was young.
Its reach is long enough
to pester a few geraniums up on the deck.

I am the god of the backyard,
who parts the waters and delivers floods
while a chipmunk rattles close by.
What's the weather forecast? Maybe enough rain coming
to make a whole rodeo of sprinklers leave town.

Snowbound

Here I am in the same place as yesterday,
panicked by snowdrifts,
happy when everyone is digging out
with their shovels high,
until they go indoors to warm up.

The landscape looked new for a day.
A week of cold weather could freeze the picture
or a thaw could reveal a familiar nothingness.

Deer Leg

Tracking hoofprints in the snow with the dog.
Later on, he brings home a detached leg.

Into the dumpster it gets hurled,
the dog circling for final traces.

We're all looking for crowns for our efforts,
showing them off like a happy mutt.

When images of folly are rebroadcast,
some can clear them away,

others return to the chase, the meat,
not sure who claims victory.

www.ingramcontent.com/pod-product-compliance
Ingram Content Group UK Ltd.
Pitfield, Milton Keynes, MK11 3LW, UK
UKHW040013200726
13854UKWH00001B/176

9 780963 309259